真⬛⬛海数学

Real Sh⬛⬛⬛⬛⬛i Mathematics

Practice Book

5.2

世纪出版

上海教育出版社
SHANGHAI EDUCATIONAL
PUBLISHING HOUSE

MIX
Paper from
responsible sources
FSC™ C007454
www.fsc.org

This book is produced from independently certified FSC™ paper to ensure responsible forest management.

For more information visit: **www.harpercollins.co.uk/green**

William Collins' dream of knowledge for all began with the publication of his first book in 1819. A self-educated mill worker, he not only enriched millions of lives, but also founded a flourishing publishing house. Today, staying true to this spirit, Collins books are packed with inspiration, innovation and practical expertise. They place you at the centre of a world of possibility and give you exactly what you need to explore it.

Collins. Freedom to teach.

Collins
An imprint of HarperCollins*Publishers*
The News Building
1 London Bridge Street
London
SE1 9GF

Browse the complete Collins catalogue at
www.collins.co.uk

Published by arrangement with Shanghai Century Publishing Group Co., Ltd.

10 9 8 7 6 5 4 3 2 1

ISBN 978-0-00-826183-2

The educational materials in this book were compiled in accordance with the course curriculum produced by the Shanghai Schools (Pre-Schools) Curriculum Reform Commission and 'Maths Syllabus for Shanghai Schools (Trial Implementation)' for use in Primary 1 First Term under the nine-year compulsory education system.

These educational materials were compiled by the head of Shanghai Normal University, and reviewed and approved for trial use by Shanghai Schools Educational Materials Review Board.

The writers for this book's educational materials are:

Editor-in-Chief: Huang Jianhong
Guest Writers: Huang Jianhong, Tong Hui, Xu Peijing

This volume's Practice Book was revised by:
'Primary School Maths Practice Book' Compilation Team

British Library Cataloguing in Publication Data
A catalogue record for this publication is available from the British Library.

For the English edition:

Primary Publishing Director: Lee Newman
Primary Publishing Managers: Fiona McGlade, Lizzie Catford
Editorial Project Manager: Mike Appleton
Editorial Manager: Amanda Harman
Editorial Assistant: Holly Blood
Managing Translator: Huang Xingfeng
Translators: Chen Qingqing, Fan Lichen, Gu Yunzi, Huang Chunhua, Lin Wenli, Lin Xumai, Lu Qingyi, Shi Zhiwei, Yang Lili, Zhao Yang
Lead Editor: Tanya Solomons
Proofreaders: Becky Moss, Life Lines Editorial Services, Joan Miller
Cover artist: Amparo Barrera
Designer: Ken Vail Graphic Design
Production Controller: Sarah Burke
Printed and bound by CPI Group (UK) Ltd, Croydon, CR0 4YY

Photo acknowledgements
The publishers wish to thank the following for permission to reproduce photographs. Every effort has been made to trace copyright holders and to obtain their permission for the use of copyright materials. The publishers will gladly receive any information enabling them to rectify any error or omission at the first opportunity.

(t = top, c = centre, b = bottom, r = right, l = left)

p45tr SHTRAUS DMYTRO/Shutterstock

All other images with permission from Shanghai Century Publishing Group.

Contents

Unit One: Revising and improving

In the Shanghai marathon, a runner completed the 42.2 km with an average speed of 16.88 km/h.

How far had this person run after 1.5 hours at this speed?

The table below lists the sections in this unit.

After completing each section, assess your work. (Use 🙂 if you are satisfied with your progress or 😐 if you are not satisfied.)

Section	Self-assessment
1. Four arithmetic operations on decimal numbers	
2. Equations	
3. Estimation of area (2)	
4. Natural numbers	

1. Four arithmetic operations on decimal numbers

Pupil Textbook pages 2–3

1. Fill in the brackets.

0.78 ÷ 0.3 = (   ) ÷ 3   18.9 ÷ 0.54 = (   ) ÷ (   )
42 ÷ 0.06 = (   ) ÷ 6   2.07 ÷ 0.23 = (   ) ÷ (   )

2. Write >, = or < in each ▢.

2.44 ▢ 2.4̇   2.4 × 0.6 ▢ 2.4   0.4 ÷ 0.6 ▢ 0.4 × 0.6
0.6̇06̇ ▢ 0.6̇0̇   2.4 ÷ 0.6 ▢ 2.4   2.4 ÷ 1.6 ▢ 2.4 × 1.6

3. Fill in the brackets.

3.6 × (   ) = 1.62   (   ) × 3.2 = 13.44   1.7 × (   ) = 8.84
9 ÷ (   ) = 2.5   (   ) ÷ 0.36 = 32.5   12.6 ÷ (   ) = 0.28

4. Use the column method to multiply and divide. Then round the numbers.

1.35 × 3.6 =   (Round to the nearest tenth.)   0.46 ÷ 4.2 =   (Round to the nearest thousandth.)

5. Work these out, showing the steps in your calculations.

1.54 + 2.02 + 3.46 + 2.98   0.25 × 7.9 × 40

2.6 × 10.1   4.23 + 4.23 × 99

$0.75 \div (0.15 \times 0.4)$ $(17.2 - 9.8 \times 0.3) \div 0.2$

$6.5 \times [14.58 - (1.7 + 1.08)]$ $9 \div [0.3 \times (1.02 + 0.18)]$

6. The table shows the amounts of water, electricity and natural gas used by Dylan's family in one month in 2016. Complete the table by calculating the costs.

			Number last month	Number this month	Units used	Unit price	Cost
Water	supply	152 tonnes	198 tonnes	___ tonnes	£1.92	£ ___
	sewage			41.4 tonnes	£1.70	£ ___
Electricity	207 kWh		367 kWh	___ kWh	£0.617	___
	89 kWh		___ kWh	___ kWh	£0.307	£15.35
Natural gas	231 cubic metres		276 cubic metres	___ cubic metres	£3.00	£ ___

1. In the Shanghai marathon, a runner completed the 42.2 km with an average speed of 16.88 km/h. How far had this person run after 1.5 hours at this speed? How long did it take to get halfway?

2. Write a two-step maths problem based on the following scenario and then try to answer it.

Dylan goes to a bookshop with £42.80 to buy a science book. The bookshop has a sale on, and the science book is now only £29.90. Dylan buys 3 notebooks with the money left.

Question: _____

_____

Answer: _____

_____

2. Equations

Pupil Textbook pages 4–5

Level **A**

1. Solve the equations and check your answers.

   a. $9x \div 3 = 1.2$

   b. $4(x + 17) \div 2 = 60$

2. Solve the equations.

   a. $12.6(x + 4.8) \div 2 = 63$

   b. $9(4.2 - x) \div 3 = 2.1$

   c. $7x + 5.5 \times 4 = 48 - 5$

   d. $3.5x \div 7 = 1$

   e. $9.5x - 5x = 5.85$

   f. $8x = 5x + 18$

g. $8(1.5x + x) = 10$

h. $2.5x + 45 - x = 60$

i. $7x - 3.2 + x = 28$

j. $2(x + x + 0.8) \div 3 = 1.2$

k. $3x = 5(x - 4)$

l. $8.4x = 4(x + 2.2)$

Guessing numbers game

I'm thinking of a number.

Take away 5 from the number in your head. Then multiply the result by 3 and divide the product by 6. What is the answer?

It's 1.5.   The number you were thinking of is 8.

How did you guess it?

3. Estimating area (2)

Pupil Textbook pages 6–7

1. Estimate the area of each shape.

a.
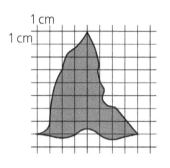

b.
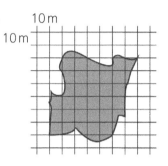

c.
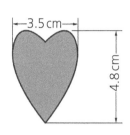

Estimate the area of each shape.

a.
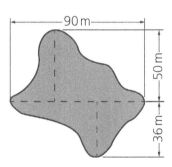

b.
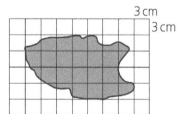

4. Natural numbers

Pupil Textbook pages 8–9

1. Fill in the brackets.

In 69, 960, 0, 3.69, 0.63, 900, 6.3̈0, 30.6, 306, 9.3̇, 60, 0.09, 6666, the natural numbers are (   ), and the decimal numbers are (   ).

2. Fill in the brackets.

a. The amount of natural numbers is (   ). (Write 'finite' or 'infinite'.)

b. In $9 + 9 + 9 + 9 + 9 = 5 \times 9$, the '5' represents (   ).

c. Write the next five natural numbers after 99:
(   ), (   ), (   ), (   ), (   ).

d. If the sum of three consecutive natural numbers is 36, the greatest of these natural numbers is (   ).

e. If the sum of three consecutive natural numbers is 111, the smallest of these natural numbers is (   ).

f. The natural numbers on either side of the natural number n are
(   ) and (   ).

3. True or false? Put a tick (✓) for 'true' or a cross (✗) for 'false' in the brackets.

a. The smallest natural number is 1.   (   )

b. The difference of two adjacent natural numbers is 1.   (   )

c. The sum of any three consecutive natural numbers is a
multiple of 3.   (   )

d. Use three number cards each of which has one number,
1, 2 or 3, to make up a three-digit number. They can make
up 6 different natural numbers.   (   )

4. What do these natural numbers represent? Write the letter of the correct answer in the brackets.

   a. The number of a student identity card is 0231, so 0231 represents (   ).

   b. If 4 sevens are added together, the 4 represents (   ).

      A. the number of repeated additions   **B.** an ordinal number

      C. a code   **D.** the final result

Look at the 100 square below and answer the following questions.

1 There are ( ) two-digit numbers in which the sum of the digits in the ones column and in the tens column is 9.

2 There are ( ) two-digit numbers in which the number in the ones column is less than the number in the tens column; there are ( ) two-digit numbers where the number in the ones column is greater than the number in the tens column.

1	2	3	4	5	6	7	8	9	10
11	12	13	14	15	16	17	18	19	20
21	22	23	24	25	26	27	28	29	30
31	32	33	34	35	36	37	38	39	40
41	42	43	44	45	46	47	48	49	50
51	52	53	54	55	56	57	58	59	60
61	62	63	64	65	66	67	68	69	70
71	72	73	74	75	76	77	78	79	80
81	82	83	84	85	86	87	88	89	90
91	92	93	94	95	96	97	98	99	100

Unit Two: Introduction to positive and negative numbers

There were 12 passengers in a train carriage, and the numbers of passengers getting on and off at two stops were +8 and −2, +3.

How many passengers are there in the carriage now? (The number of passengers getting on is positive, and the number of passengers getting off is negative.)

The table below lists the sections in this unit.

After completing each section, assess your work. (Use 😊 if you are satisfied with your progress or 😐 if you are not satisfied.)

Section	Self-assessment
1. Positive and negative numbers	
2. Number lines	

1. Positive and negative numbers

Pupil Textbook pages 11–16

Level **A**

1. **Of the following numbers, which are positive and which are negative? Write them in the corresponding ovals.**

$$-1 \qquad 3.8 \qquad +\frac{1}{2} \qquad 0 \qquad -3.58 \qquad 123 \qquad -4.95$$

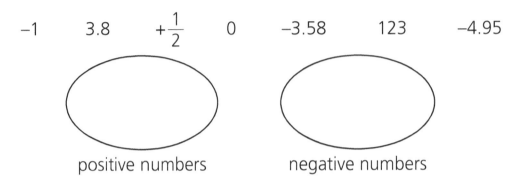

positive numbers   negative numbers

2. **Read each thermometer, then write the temperature shown on it in the brackets below. Then read it again.**

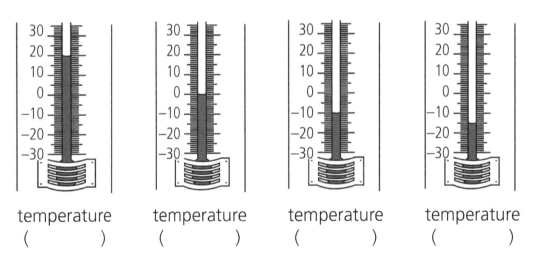

temperature   temperature   temperature   temperature
(   )   (   )   (   )   (   )

3. **Fill in the brackets.**

   a. The Moon's surface temperature during the day can be as high as 126 degrees above zero degrees Celsius, and this can be recorded as (   )°C; the night temperature drops to 150 degrees below zero degrees Celsius, and this can be recorded as (   )°C.

   b. 28°C above zero refers to 28 degrees (   ) than 0°C; 5 degrees below zero refers to 5 degrees (   ) than 0°C. (Write 'higher' or 'lower' in the brackets.)

c. Numbers such as +5, +12.8, +0.36 with a + in front are (   )
and the + sign in front of the positive number (   )
be omitted; numbers such as –6, –9.98, with a (   )
sign in front, are negative, and the negative sign (   )
be omitted.

4. Colour each thermometer to show the lowest temperature in each city for one day in December. One has been done for you. Shanghai: –2 °C; Beijing: –8 °C; Guangzhou: 6 °C; Hangzhou: 0 °C.

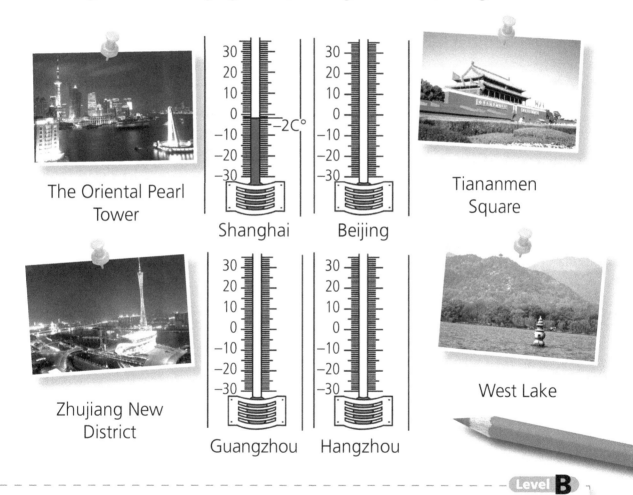

The Oriental Pearl Tower

Shanghai   Beijing

Tiananmen Square

Zhujiang New District

Guangzhou   Hangzhou

West Lake

Level **B**

The world's highest peak is Mount Everest at 8844.43 metres above sea level, which is written as +8844.43 metres. The Mariana Trench in the Pacific is 11 034 metres below sea level, which is written as (   ) metres; The height difference between the top of Mount Everest and the bottom of the Mariana Trench is (   ) metres.

1. **Draw lines to match each statement with its inverse or opposite statement.**

   Increase by 2 percentage points   Decrease by 15 degrees Celsius
   17 people getting off   Take out £1500
   Rise by 15 degrees Celsius   17 people getting on
   Deposit £1500   Fall by 2 percentage points

2. **Qinghai Lake, which is found northeast of Qinghai Province, is the largest lake in China and is 3196 metres above sea level. The lake is recorded as being at an altitude of (   ) metres. The world's highest navigable freshwater lake, which is in South America, is 3812 metres above sea level. It is recorded as being at an altitude of (   ) metres. The world's lowest body of water is the Dead Sea in Israel. It is 400 metres below sea level, and is recorded as being at an altitude of (   ) metres.**

3. **The table shows Poppy's family's income and payments in April. Use positive and negative numbers to complete the final column. (Income is denoted as a positive number.)**

Date	Abstracts	Income and payments (units: £)
5 April	Father's salary was £3700.	+3700
6 April	The cost of water, electricity and natural gas was £290.	−290
12 April	The telephone bill was £130.	
15 April	Mother's salary was £3500.	
20 April	Mother spent £620 on clothes.	
28 April	The whole family went out for the day and spent £800.	
30 April	Cost of food for this month was £1780.	

4. If the water level increases by 3 metres we record this as +3 metres, then if the water level drops by 3 metres we record it as (   ) metres; if the water level does not rise or fall, then we can record it as (   ) metres.

5. Emma goes north for –50 metres, which means she actually goes (   ) for 50 metres.

6. The natural forest protection project was implemented from 2000 to 2011. The table shows the changes in the forest area of Inner Mongolia (10 000 mu), the forest stock (100 million cubic metres), and the amount of sediment that flows into the Yellow River (million tonnes/year). If an increase is stated as positive, use positive and negative numbers to indicate their growth and fall in the following table.

Natural forest resources protection project (Inner Mongolia project area)	Growth	Recorded as
Forest area (10 000 mu)	An increase of 46.16 million mu	
Forest stock (100 million cubic metres)	An increase of 175 million cubic metres	
The amount of sediment that enters the yellow river (10 000 tonnes / year)	A reduction of 37 million tonnes/year	

Note: 46.16 million mu = 30.773 billion square metres.

7. **The standard water level of a reservoir is recorded as 0 metres and the height of the water above the standard water level is indicated by positive numbers.**

   a. A water level lower than the standard level by 0.1 metres can be recorded as (   ); a water level that is 0.2 metres higher than the standard can be recorded as (   ).

   b. 0.18 metres means the water is (   ) than the standard water level by 0.18 metres; –0.23 metres indicates that the water level is (   ) than the standard water level by 0.23 metres.

Level B

This diagram represents a line from west to east, divided into metres. (East is the positive direction.) Each division represents 1 metre. Alex is standing at the start, at 0 metres.

West   East

–6 –5 –4 –3 –2 –1 0 1 2 3 4 5 6

a. If Alex goes east for 5 metres from point 0, recorded as +5 metres, and then walks west for 3 metres from point 0, this will be recorded as (   ) metres.

b. If Alex's position is +6 metres, this means he has gone from point 0 to the (   ) on the line by (   ) metres.

c. If Alex's position is –4 metres, this means he has gone from point 0 to the (   ) on the line by (   ) metres.

d. Alex sets out from point 0, and goes east for 2 metres, and then 4 metres to the west. Alex's final position can be recorded as (   ) metres.

e. If Alex starts from point 0, first he goes west for 10 metres, and then 18 metres to east. So Alex's final position is recorded as (   ) metres.

As shown in the diagram below, Dylan, Alex and their school are on the same line. The location of the school is marked 0, and the direction east of the school is taken as positive. The length between each grid mark is 200 metres.

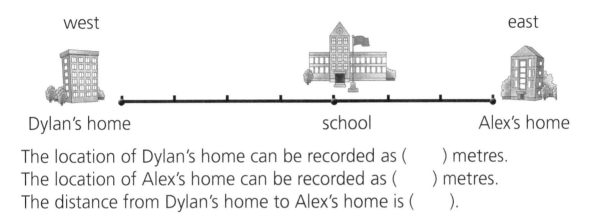

west   east

Dylan's home   school   Alex's home

The location of Dylan's home can be recorded as (   ) metres.
The location of Alex's home can be recorded as (   ) metres.
The distance from Dylan's home to Alex's home is (   ).

1. Dylan and his mother went to a shopping mall. They parked the car in the car park on the ground floor, and then took the lift to the 5th floor to watch a film. After watching the film, they took the lift and went down to the 3rd floor to buy some toys. At this moment, they had travelled (   ) floors in the lift.

A. 8   **B.** 9

C. 5   **D.** 7

Note: if you take the lift from the 2nd floor to the 4th floor, you go up 2 floors.

2. Emma's dad was coming back from Manchester on a business trip, and he was planning to take the Metrolink home. He got on at Piccadilly Gardens station. There were 12 passengers in the carriage when he got on, including himself. At each stop, he counted the number of people getting on and off. (The number of passengers getting on is recorded as a positive number and the number of passengers getting off is recorded as a negative number.)

Name of station	Changes in the number of passengers	Number of passengers in the carriage
Market Street	+8 people	20 people
Shudehill	−2 people, +3 people	
Victoria	−1 person	
Queens Road	+9 people	
Abraham Moss	−10 people, +6 people	
Crumpsall	−2 people, +4 people	
……	……	

From the record of passengers getting on and off, count the number of passengers in the carriage before arriving at Crumpsall station.

a. Altogether, (   ) passengers got on.

b. Altogether, (   ) passengers got off.

c. At this time, there were (   ) passengers in the carriage.

2. Number lines

Pupil Textbook pages 17–20

Level **A**

1. A straight line with an (   ), a positive (   ) and a unit (   ) is a number line.

2. Look at the number line and write the answers.

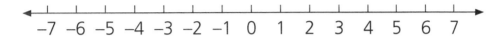

a. The point +6 is to the (   ) side of the origin and (   ) units from the origin.

b. The point −3 is to the (   ) side of the origin and (   ) units from the origin.

c. The point (   ) is to the left of the origin and 7 units away from the origin.

d. The point (   ) is to the right of the origin and 2.5 units away from the origin.

e. On the (   ) side of the origin, the point (   ) units from the origin is −5.

f. On the (   ) side of the origin, the point (   ) units from the origin is 5.

3. Write the number that each point, *A*, *B*, *C*, *D* and *E*, represents.

D   A   B E   C

−4 −3 −2 −1 0 1 2 3 4

The number represented by point *A* is (   ); the number represented by point *B* is (   ); the number represented by point *C* is (   ); the number represented by point *D* is (   ); the number represented by point *E* is (   ).

4. Use the number line to compare these numbers. (Write >, = or < in each ◯.)

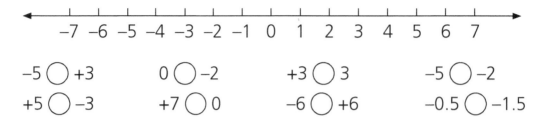

-5 ◯ +3   0 ◯ -2   +3 ◯ 3   -5 ◯ -2

+5 ◯ -3   +7 ◯ 0   -6 ◯ +6   -0.5 ◯ -1.5

5. Find and compare.

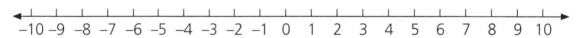

a. Find and mark the points for –8, +1, –6, 0, +10, +8 and –6.5 on the number line, and label them *A*, *B*, *C*, *D*, *E*, *F* and *G*.

b. Compare the numbers in part **a.** on the number line above, and write them in order from smallest to greatest.

_____

c. Of the above numbers, the whole numbers that are less than 4 but greater than –4 are (   ).

6. Compare the following numbers and write them in order from smallest to greatest.

–5, +23, 0, +3, –2.5, –1

_____

7. Look at the number line and fill in the brackets.

```
        A        B    C        D        E  F
  ◀──┼──┼──┼──┼──┼──┼──┼──┼──┼──┼──┼──┼──┼──┼──▶
    -7 -6 -5 -4 -3 -2 -1  0  1  2  3  4  5  6  7
```

a. Point *D* is (   ) unit(s) away from the origin and point *E* is
   (   ) unit(s) away from the origin. The distance between them is
   (   ) unit(s).

b. Point A is (　　) unit(s) away from the origin and point C is (　　) unit(s) away from the origin. The distance between them is (　　) unit(s).

c. Point B is (　　) unit(s) away from the origin and point D is (　　) unit(s) away from the origin. The distance between them is (　　) unit(s).

d. Point F is (　　) unit(s) away from the origin and point A is (　　) unit(s) away from the origin. The distance between them is (　　) unit(s).

8. Multiple choice – write the letter of the correct answer in the brackets.

a. On the number line, the point(s) 1 unit away from the origin is/are (　　).

   A. +1　　**B.** –1　　**C.** 0　　**D.** +1 and –1

b. On the number line, if the point M is on the left side of N, then the relationship between M and N is (　　).

   A. $M < N$　　**B.** $M > N$　　**C.** $M = N$　　**D.** uncertain

Level **B**

Write +4, 0, –3, +1, +5, –5 and –1 in the correct places in this diagram.

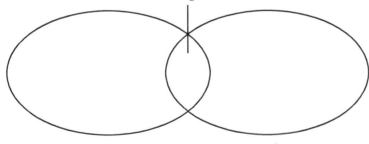

less than 2 but greater than –2

less than 2　　　　greater than –2

Unit Three: Simple equations (2)

How many children are there altogether? How many pieces are there in this puzzle?

Some children are working together to complete a jigsaw. If each child takes 200 pieces, there are 600 pieces left. If each child takes 300 pieces, they can complete the puzzle.

The table below lists the sections in this unit.
After completing each section, assess your work. (Use 😊 if you are satisfied with your progress or 😐 if you are not satisfied.)

Section	Self-assessment
1. Problem solving with equations (3)	
2. Problem solving with equations (4)	

1. Problem solving with equations (3)

Problem solving with equations

a. The perimeter of this rectangle is 76 centimetres. The length is 26 centimetres, so what is its width, in centimetres?

26 cm

b. In the park, the ground was paved with several blocks of parallelogram-shaped tiles for a new game called Plaza. The area of each tile is 468 square centimetres, and the length of the base is 26 centimetres (as shown in the diagram). What is the height of the tile, in centimetres?

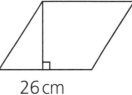

26 cm

c. Use Dylan and Poppy's statement to calculate the top base of the trapezium, in centimetres.

4 cm

10 cm

The area of the right-angled trapezium is 32 square centimetres.

The bottom base of the right-angled trapezium is 10 centimetres, and its height is 4 centimetres.

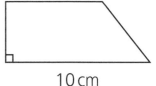

d. A rectangular garden is 4 metres long. Half of the area is planted with yellow tulips, and half is planted with red roses (as shown by the shaded area in the diagram). The area for growing roses is 4 square metres. What is the width of this rectangular garden, in metres?

4 m

e. Emma combines a parallelogram with a triangle to make a trapezium, as shown in the diagram. The area of the trapezium is 116 square centimetres, and the base and height of the parallelogram are both 8 centimetres. How long is the bottom base of the trapezium, in centimetres?

←8 cm→

8 cm

? cm

Level **B**

As shown in the diagram, if one edge of a square is increased by 5 cm, and the other edge is increased by 8 cm, the area of the rectangular area is then increased by 170 cm². What was the area of the original square? (Use equations to solve the problem.)

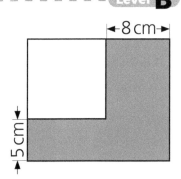

←8 cm→

5 cm

Problem solving with equations

a. There are some books in the corner of the classroom. The relationship between the number of fairy tale books and science books is as follows:

Fairy tale books ⌐____⌐
Science books ⌐____⌐____⌐____⌐ ⎫ a total of 56 books

How many fairy tale books and how many science books are there in the corner of the classroom?

b. In a nature reserve, there are swans and red-crowned cranes. There are 960 birds altogether. The number of swans is 2.2 times the number of red-crowned cranes. How many swans and how many red-crowned cranes are there?

c. Two teams worked together to build a 4-kilometre road. The length built by team A was 1.5 times the length built by team B. How many kilometres of road did each team build?

d. As shown in the diagram, angle 1 and angle 2 added together make a right angle; angle 2 is twice the size (in degrees) of angle 1. What are the sizes of angles 1 and 2?

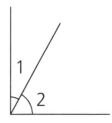

Level **B**

Emma made a rectangle from 2 identical squares. The perimeter of her rectangle was 19.2 cm. How long were the sides of the squares? (Use equations to solve the problem.)

Problem solving with equations

a. Mum bought a fridge-freezer and a washing machine. Use the line segment diagram to work out the costs of the fridge-freezer and the washing machine.

The fridge-freezer costs £1050 more than the washing machine

Price of the washing machine

Price of the fridge-freezer

b. A school arranged for its pupils to visit a 'How to eat healthily' exhibition. 24 more pupils went from Year 5 than Year 4, and this was 1.2 times the number of pupils from Year 4. How many pupils went from Year 4? How many went from Year 5?

c. The total area of the oceans is about 2.4 times the area of land on the surface of the Earth. This is 210 million square kilometres more than the area of land. How many million square kilometres are there of ocean and of land?

d. The fruit shop bought watermelons and apples from their supplier. The mass of the watermelons was 90 kilograms more than that of the apples. The mass of the watermelons was 3 times that of the apples. How many kilograms of watermelons and of apples were there?

The difference of *A* minus *B* is 56. *A* divided by *B* gives 7 and the remainder is 2. What are these two numbers? (Use equations to solve the problem.)

Problem solving with equations

a. Alex and Dylan are typing together. Look at the line segment diagram and answer: How many words did Alex type and how many did Dylan type?

120 more words

Alex └────────────────┤
Dylan └──────────────────┘

2000 words altogether

b. Poppy took £50 to the stationery shop. She spent £10.80 pounds more than she had left. How much did the stationery items cost?

c. Emma cuts a 1 metre strip of paper into two pieces, with a difference in length of 18 cm. How long is each of these two pieces of paper, in centimetres?

d. The sum of three consecutive natural numbers is 204. What are the three numbers?

Level **B**

During the midterm examinations, Dylan's average of his scores for English and Maths was 87.5, and his score for English was 9 marks lower than that for Maths. How many marks did Dylan get for English and how many for Maths? (Use equations to solve the problem.)

Problem solving with equations

a. A basket of oranges weighs 1.8 kilograms, and the oranges are 1040 grams heavier than the basket. How many grams of oranges are there, and how many grams does the basket weigh?

b. In a badminton match, the number of male fans is 3 times the number of female fans, plus 156. The number of male fans is 504 more than the number of female fans. How many male and how many female fans are there?

c. Poppy and Emma saved their pocket money, and put it in the bank. They saved a total of £2600. The amount Poppy saved is £200 less than 2.5 times the amount Emma saved. How much money did Poppy deposit in the bank?

d. In total, 3 pieces of iron plate weigh 210 kilograms. The first piece is twice as heavy as the second, and the third is 4 times as heavy as the second. What is the mass of each of the 3 pieces of iron?

Level B

Problem solving with equations

a. Using the clues given by Emma and Dylan, answer: How many chickens and how many rabbits are there in the enclosure?

The numbers of chickens and rabbits in the enclosure are the same.

They have 48 legs altogether.

b. As shown in the diagram, a square with 10 cm sides is divided into a triangle and a trapezium. The area of the trapezium is 20 square centimetres larger than that of the triangle. What is the area of the triangle?

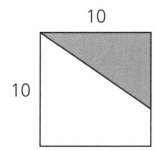

10

10

Problem solving with equations

a. The distance by road between London and Edinburgh is about 660 kilometres. A truck leaves London headed for Edinburgh and a bus leaves Edinburgh headed for London at the same time. The truck travels at an average speed of 48 km/h. The bus travels at an average speed of 72 km/h. After how many hours do the truck and the bus pass each other?

b. A document has 5700 words. As it is needed urgently, two typists, Anna and Bella, start typing at the same time. Anna types 100 words per minute, on average, and Bella types 90 words per minute, on average. How long do they take to finish the document?

c. The distance between two cities, by road, is 624.5 kilometres. A bus starts from one city and a truck starts from the other city at the same time and they travel towards each other. After 5 hours, the bus and the truck pass each other. The bus travels at 70 kilometres per hour, on average. What is the speed of the truck?

d. Emma and her mum fold 'lucky stars' together. Her mum folded 64 each day, on average, and Emma folded 31 each day, on average. How many days did they take to fold 380 'lucky stars'?

e. A car and a bus start from the same place at the same time, travelling on the same road in opposite directions. The car travels at 95 kilometres per hour, on average. The bus travels at 80 kilometres per hour, on average. After how many hours are they 350 kilometres apart?

Level **B**

Miss Smith and Mr Jones set off from the same place by bike and ride in opposite directions. Mr Jones rides at 12 kilometres per hour. Mr Jones is 1 kilometre per hour faster than Miss Smith. After how many hours are they 15 kilometres apart? (Use equations to solve the problem.)

Problem solving with equations

a. Boat A and boat B set out from the same harbour at different times. After boat A had sailed 4.5 km, boat B set out. Boat A sailed at 24.5 km/h on average, and boat B sailed at 27.5 km/h. After how long will boat B catch up with boat A? (Write the details in the bar model and then solve the problem.)

Suppose: boat B will catch up with boat A in x hours.

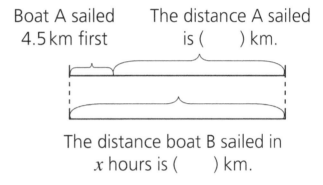

Boat A sailed 4.5 km first   The distance A sailed is ( ) km.

The distance boat B sailed in x hours is ( ) km.

b. Alex and Emma both go to the cinema after school. They set out, along the same road, one after the other. Alex left after Emma had walked 50 metres. Emma walked at 67 metres per minute, on average, and Alex caught up with her after 10 minutes. How far did Alex walk per minute, on average?

c. In a PE lesson, Alex stands at the starting point of a 100-metre track. Dylan stands 10 metres in front of him and they run in the same direction. Alex runs at 5 metres per second, on average, and Dylan runs at 4.5 metres per second, on average. After how long does Alex catch up with Dylan?

d. The children in Year 5 Class 1 are divided into 2 groups to fold paper cranes. After the first group had folded 30 cranes, the second group started to fold them as well. After 30 minutes, the number of paper cranes folded by the second group was the same as the number folded by the first group. If the first group folded 12 paper cranes per minute, how many paper cranes did the second group fold per minute, on average?

e. A motorbike sets out from city A towards city B, travelling at 40 kilometres per hour. One hour later, a car sets out from city A towards city B, along the same road, travelling at 80 kilometres per hour, on average. After how long will the car catch up with the motorbike?

Level **B**

Write equations to solve the problems.

a. Poppy's home is 1.3 kilometres from her school. Poppy walks to school at 62 metres per minute in the morning. After Poppy had walked 440 metres, her mother noticed that Poppy had forgotten to take her pencil case, so her mother ran after her at 150 metres per minute, and caught up with her. How long did it take her to catch up with Poppy? How far was Poppy from school at that point?

b. Two runners, Arran and Barry, start to run from the same place in the same direction along a 400-metre track. Arran runs at 280 metres per minute, on average, and Barry runs 240 metres per minute, on average. How long will it take for Arran to run one lap more than Barry?

Write equations to solve the problems.

a. The teacher is arranging dormitories for pupils attending an adventure camp. If 8 pupils sleep in each dormitory, there will be exactly enough dormitories; if 6 pupils sleep in each dormitory, 4 more dormitories would be needed. How many dormitories are there? How many pupils are there?

b. Emma plans to read a book over a number of days. If she reads 20 pages each day, she will finish the book by the last day; if she reads 18 pages each day, she will need one more day to finish it. How long does Emma need to finish reading the book? How many pages does the book have?

c. Alex uses disc holders to tidy up his DVDs. If he puts 30 in each disc holder, there are exactly enough holders. If he puts 40 discs in each holder, one will be empty. How many disc holders did he have? How many discs did he have?

d. A factory is producing a new style of mobile phone. If it produces 40 thousand phones every day, then the order will be completed exactly when it is needed. If it produces 43 thousand every day, then the order will be completed 9 days before it is needed. How many days are needed to complete the order on time? How many mobile phones are there?

Write equations to solve the problems.

a. Dylan leaves home at 7.30 every morning to walk to school. If he walks at a speed of 70 metres per minute, he arrives at school exactly on time. If he walks at 60 metres per minute, he is exactly 5 minutes late. Is 8.00 the time school starts?

b. As shown in the diagram, an ant and a snail walk in different directions from point A, starting at the same time. The speed of the ant is 0.5 metres per minute, and the speed of the snail is 0.3 metres per minute.

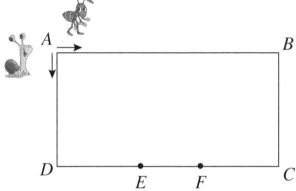

i. When the ant arrives at point C, the snail just arrives at point E, which is 1.2 metres from point C. How long have they been walking for?

ii. When the snail meets the ant at point F for the first time, how far will they have walked?

2. Problem solving with equations (4)

Pupil Textbook pages 33–40

Level **A**

Write equations to solve the problems.

a. The distance between towns A and B, by road, is 500 kilometres. A truck and a car set off from A and B respectively, at the same time, travelling towards each other and will meet on the way. The two vehicles have still not met after 3 hours and their distance apart is 89 kilometres. If the truck travels at an average speed of 62 kilometres per hour, what is the average speed of the car?

b. The length of the railway between two cities is 1500 kilometres. A train sets off from each of the two cities travelling towards each other and they will meet on the way. The slower train travels at 82 kilometres per hour, on average, and the faster train travels at 106 kilometres per hour, on average. The faster train travels for 90 kilometres before the slower train sets off. After how long will the slower train meet the faster train?

c. The distance between towns A and B, by road, is 590 kilometres. A van left A and a car left B at the same time, intending to meet each other along the way. The van broke down and it took 1.2 hours for it to be repaired. The car met the van 4 hours after they both set out. The car travelled at 95 kilometres per hour, on average. What was the speed of the van on average?

d. Alex's home is directly west of their school, Poppy's home is directly east of their school, and the distance between their homes is 1170 metres. Alex walks at 75 metres per minute, on average, and Poppy walks at 70 metres per minute, on average. If Alex walks 300 metres towards the school before Poppy leaves home, they will arrive at school at the same time. How long does Poppy take to walk to school? How far is Alex's home from the school?

Write equations to solve the problems.

a. The distance from Aunt Jane's house to Uncle Peter's house is 7.95 kilometres. Aunt Jane and Uncle Peter decide to meet each other. Aunt Jane sets out at 2:00 on foot, walking at 0.07 kilometres per minute, on average. Uncle Peter sets out at 2:30 by bike, and they meet 15 minutes after he leaves. What is Uncle Peter's average speed, in kilometres per minute?

b. Two harbours are 758 kilometres apart. Two ships, A and B, set out at the same time and plan to meet each other. Ship A sails at 35 kilometres per hour, on average, and ship B sails at 37 kilometres per hour, on average. One hour after leaving, Ship A is recalled to its harbour to pick up an important passenger. It then leaves immediately to meet ship B. How long after they first set out will the ships meet?

Write equations to solve the problems.

a. Dylan left home to go to the park, walking at 72 metres per minute. Eight minutes after he left, his father left home on a bicycle to catch him up. His speed was 264 metres per minute. How many minutes will it take Dylan's father to catch up with Dylan?

b. Poppy and Emma agreed to meet at the amusement park. They both left school at the same time, but Poppy went to the supermarket to buy a drink on the way, so she was delayed by 5 minutes. Poppy and Emma both arrived at the amusement park 20 minutes after they left school. Emma's speed was 57 metres per minute. What was Poppy's speed?

c. At the weekend, Alex walked to his grandpa's home, 2 km away. Alex's speed was 62 metres per minute. After 20 minutes, Grandpa started out to meet Alex. His speed was 90 metres per minute. After how many minutes did they meet?

d. A motorbike and a bicycle set out, at the same time, from two places that were 290 km apart. They travelled towards each other. The speed of the motorbike was 55 kilometres per hour. During the journey, the chain of the bicycle broke and it took half an hour to be repaired. As a result, the motorbike met the bicycle 4 hours after it started. What was the speed of the bicycle when it was travelling?

Write equations to solve the problems.

a. After meeting for lunch, Albert and Benny set off to drive home, in opposite directions. After half an hour, Albert noticed he had Benny's phone, so he turned around immediately to catch his friend. If Albert's speed was 80 kilometres per hour and Benny's speed was 60 kilometres per hour, after how long will Albert catch up with Benny?

b. Two cars drove from A to B. The speed of the faster car was 102 kilometres per hour and the speed of the slower car was 85 kilometres per hour. The slower car started 1 hour after the faster car. When the faster car arrives at B, the slower car is 204 km away from B. At this time, for how many hours has the slower car travelled? What is the distance between A and B, in kilometres?

Write equations to solve the problems.

a. A bag contains equal numbers of red glass balls and blue glass balls. Five red balls and three blue balls were taken from the bag. This was repeated several times. When the red balls ran out, 12 blue balls remained in the bag. How many times were glass balls taken out? How many red and how many blue glass balls were in the bag to start with?

b. The apples in a basket are shared equally among some children. If each child gets 2 apples, there are 24 apples left. If each child gets 5 apples, there are no apples left. How many children are there in total? How many apples were in the basket?

c. Some children are working together to complete a jigsaw. If each child takes 200 pieces, there are 600 pieces left over. If each child takes 300 pieces, they can complete the puzzle. How many children are there altogether? How many pieces are there in this puzzle?

d. Dylan went to the fruit shop to buy some grapes. If he buys 2.5 kg, he will have £2.58 left. If he buys 4 kg, he will have no money left. How much does each kilogram of grapes cost? How much money did Dylan take to the shop?

e. The pupils of Year 5 Class 1 are helping the school cook to put sausage rolls into boxes. If they put 6 sausage rolls in each box, they will use 72 fewer sausage rolls than the cook has made. If they put 8 sausage rolls in each box, they will use all the sausage rolls. Each pupil packs one box. How many pupils are there in Year 5 Class 1? How many sausage rolls were made in total?

Write equations to solve the problems.

a. Two cars, A and B, started from two places at the same time and travelled towards each other. After car A had travelled 260 km, it met car B. At this time, car A was 30 km past the midpoint between the two places. Given that the speed of car B was 80 kilometres per hour, for how many hours had car B travelled when they met?

b. A box contains black counters and white counters. There are twice as many black counters as white counters. Groups of four black and three white counters were taken from the box. When the last three white counters were removed, 18 black counters remained. How many groups of counters were removed? How many black counters and how many white counters were there?

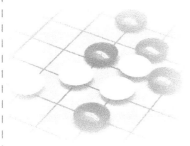

Unit Four: Let's practise geometry

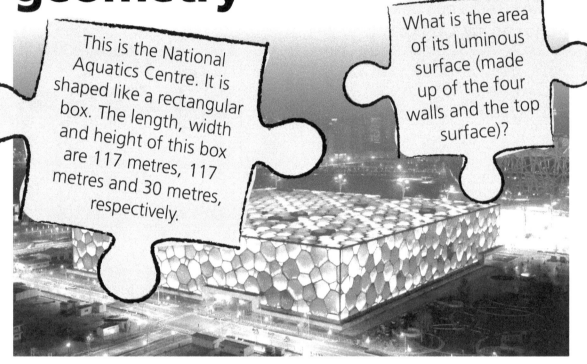

This is the National Aquatics Centre. It is shaped like a rectangular box. The length, width and height of this box are 117 metres, 117 metres and 30 metres, respectively.

What is the area of its luminous surface (made up of the four walls and the top surface)?

The table below lists the sections in this unit.

After completing each section, assess your work. (Use 😊 if you are satisfied with your progress or 😐 if you are not satisfied.)

Section	Self-assessment
1. Volume	
2. Cubic centimetres and cubic metres	
3. Understanding cuboids and cubes	
4. Volume of cuboids and cubes	
5. Volume of combined 3D shapes	
6. Nets of cuboids and cubes	
7. Surface areas of cuboids and cubes	
8. Practice exercise	
9. Changes in surface area	
10. Volume and capacity	
11. Volume and mass	

1. Volume

Pupil Textbook pages 42–44

1. Fill in the blanks.

a. The space occupied by an object is called the object's (   ).

b. In the picture, the orange is larger, so the space it occupies is also
(   ). The grape is smaller, so the space it occupies is also
(   ).

c. The orange occupies more space than the
grape, so the orange's (   ) is greater
than the grape's.

2. A direct comparison of volume

a. The two cakes are the same height. Do they have the same
volume? Explain your answer.

b. These two sticks have the same thickness. Do they
have the same volume? Explain your answer.

c. The length of these two rectangular bars is the same. Do they
have the same volume? Explain your answer.

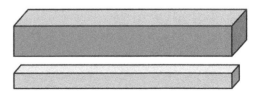

3. Will the total volume be changed in the following conditions?

   a. The whole of a cuboid iron block is made into an iron cube, so its shape has changed.
   Has its volume changed?

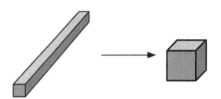

   b. A cake is cut into slices. Has the volume of cake changed?

4. Look at the story and write 'yes' or 'no'.

   The crow is trying to drink the water in the bottle. Think about what happens as the crow puts stones into the bottle. Is there any change in the volume of water in the bottle? (   )

Level **B**

Short exercise

Design a simple experiment to show that even when the shape of an object changes its volume does not. For example, when you pour water from a bowl into a bottle, the height of the water changes, but the volume does not.

2. Cubic centimetres and cubic metres

Pupil Textbook pages 45–49

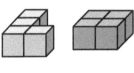

1. Fill in the brackets.

a. The length of the edge of a cube is 1 centimetre, so its volume is ( ). The three-dimensional (3D) shape consists of ( ) centimetre cubes and its volume is ( ).

b. The volume of each cube is 1 cubic centimetre. The volumes of *A* and *B* in the 3D shape are the ( ). (Fill in the brackets with 'same' or 'different'.)

A   *B*

2. The volume of each cube is 1 cubic centimetre. What are the volumes of these 3D shapes?

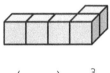

( ) cm³   ( ) cm³   ( ) cm³

3. How many centimetre cubes make up the cuboid and cube below? What is the volume of each?

There are ( ) centimetre cubes in all.
Its volume is ( ) cm³

There are ( ) centimetre cubes in all.
Its volume is ( ) cm³

Level B

How many centimetre cubes make up the 3D shape on the right? What is its volume?

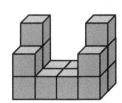

1. Fill in the brackets.

    a. A cube has an edge length of 1 centimetre, so its volume is ( ). A cube has an edge length of 1 metre, so its volume is ( ).

    b. A cube has an edge length of 10 centimetres, so it consists of ( ) centimetre cubes. A cube has an edge length of 1 metre, so it consists of ( ) centimetre cubes.

    c. A cube has an edge length of 4 centimetres, so it consists of ( ) centimetre cubes and its volume is ( ).

    d. A cube has an edge length of 3 metres, so it consists of ( ) centimetre cubes and its volume is ( ).

2. Conversions between units of cubic centimetres and cubic metres

    a. $6 \, cm^3 = $ _____ mm^3 $7600 \, cm^3 = $ _____ m^3

         $0.53 \, cm^3 = $ _____ mm^3 $89 \, cm^3 = $ _____ m^3

    b. $26 \, m^3 = $ _____ cm^3 $14000 \, mm^3 = $ _____ cm^3

         $0.018 \, m^3 = $ _____ cm^3 $70 \, mm^3 = $ _____ cm^3

    c. $9 \, m^3 = $ _____ cm^3 $0.02 \, m^3 = $ _____ cm^3

    d. $10020 \, cm^3 = $ _____ m^3 $10.1 \, m^3 = $ _____ cm^3

1. Conversions between units of cubic centimetres and cubic metres.

     $2 \, m^3 \, 2 \, cm^3 = $ _____ cm^3 $15 \, m^3 \, 500 \, cm^3 = $ _____ m^3

2. Look at some real objects carefully. Which objects measure about 1 cubic centimetre or 1 cubic metre?

3. Understanding cuboids and cubes

Level **A**

1. Fill in the brackets.

a. i. A cuboid is a 3D shape enclosed by (   ) rectangular faces.

ii. In a cuboid, the shapes of the opposing faces are (   ), the sizes are (   ) and the length of the parallel edges are (   ).

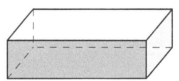

iii. In a cuboid, the length of the three edges that intersect at one vertex are called the cuboid's (   ), (   ) and (   ).

b. i. A cuboid with length, width and height the same is called a (   ).

ii. The six faces of the cube are square, and the area of these six squares is (   ).

c. Cuboids and cubes both have (   ) faces, (   ) edges and (   ) vertices.

d. A cube's edge length is 2.4 metres, so the edges have a total length of (   ).

e. The length of a cuboid is 3 cm, the width is 2 cm and the height is 1 cm. So, the total length of the edges is (   ) cm.

2. What is the relationship between cuboids and cubes? Draw a diagram to show the relationship between them.

1. Fill in the brackets.

a. A cuboid's width is 20 centimetres, its height is 100 centimetres and the total length of its edges is 8 metres. The length of this cuboid is (   ) centimetres.

b. The total edge length of a cuboid is 48 metres, its length is 1.5 times its height and its height is 2 times its width. The length of the cuboid is (   ) metres, the width is (   ) metres and the height is (   ) metres.

2. Short exercise

Use 12 small cubes of the same size to build a cuboid and record the cuboid's length, width and height in the table below. (Try to make three different cuboids.)

Cuboid	Length	Width	Height
1			
2			
3			

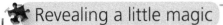

Explaining 'The magic of guessing a number' on page 105

No matter which digits Dylan chooses at the beginning, as long as Poppy divides the 10th digit reported by 0.618, she can work out the digit in the 11th box.

For example, the digits Dylan chose first and second were 3 and 4. Using the steps of the magic, we can fill in the next digits, as shown below.

| 3 | 4 | 7 | 11 | 18 | 29 | 47 | 76 | 123 | 199 | ? |

Dylan says to Poppy, 'My 10th digit is 199.'

Poppy uses the calculator to divide the number Dylan tells her by 0.618, and the result is 322. This is the number that should be in the 11th box!

At the beginning of the magic trick, we agreed that the range of the numbers was 1 to 10. However, this is only for the convenience of the calculation, but the magic is also possible with numbers that are outside this range.

As for the mathematical reason behind the magic, you'll be able to solve the mystery when you learn more about fractions at school.

4. Volume of cuboids and cubes

Pupil Textbook pages 52–54

Level A

1. Conversions

$3.2\,m^3 = ($ $)\,cm^3$

$78.06\,m^3 = ($ $)\,cm^3$

$5\,m^3 = ($ $)\,cm^3$

$36\,502\,cm^3 = ($ $)\,m^3$

$406\,000\,cm^3 = ($ $)\,m^3$

$($ $)\,dm^3 = 4050\,cm^3$

2. Fill in the brackets with suitable units of volume (cubic centimetres or cubic metres).

The volume of a garden pond is about 4 ( ).

The volume of an apple is about 100 ( ).

The volume of a box of chocolates is about 2500 ( ).

3. If we want to work out the volume of a cuboid with a length of 6 cm, a width of 4 cm and a height of 3 cm, we can use centimetre cubes to help us.

First, we can use the cubes to show the length by putting ( ) centimetre cubes in a row on the floor.

Then, we can use the cubes to show the width by putting ( ) centimetre cubes in a row on the floor.

Finally, we can use the cubes to show the height by putting ( ) centimetre cubes in a row on the floor.

Because in this cuboid there are ( ) centimetre cubes in all, its volume is ( ) cubic centimetre(s).

4. Work out the volumes of the cuboid and cube below.

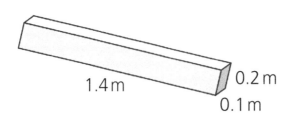

1.4 m   0.2 m
0.1 m

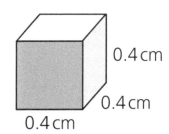

0.4 cm
0.4 cm
0.4 cm

5. The shape of a hardback book is a cuboid. Its length is 28 cm, its width is 18 cm and its thickness is 4 cm. What is the volume of the book, in cubic centimetres?

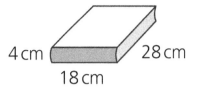

6. Look at the 3D shapes and find the unknowns.

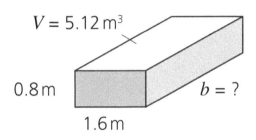

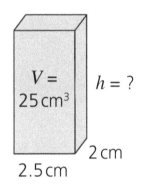

Level **B**

A cube of steel has a length of 40 cm. If we reshape it into a cuboid of steel 20 cm in height and width, how many centimetres will the length of the steel be? (Ignore any loss in the reshaping.)

5. Volume of combined 3D shapes

Pupil Textbook page 55

Work out the volume of each combined 3D shape. (units: cm)

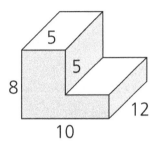

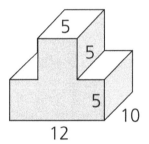

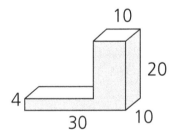

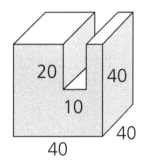

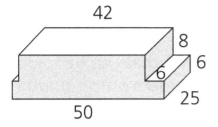

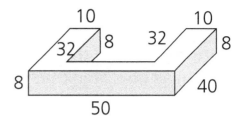

1. Work out the volume of this combined 3D shape. (units: cm)

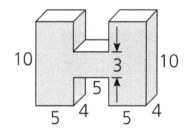

2. Work out the volume of this combined 3D shape. (units: cm)

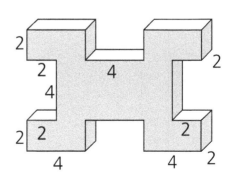

6. Nets of cuboids and cubes

Pupil Textbook pages 56–57

1. Write a tick (✓) in the brackets for each net that can be folded to form a cube. Think first and then copy them onto squared paper and try folding them.

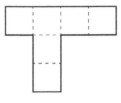

a. (   )

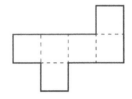

b. (   )

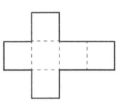

c. (   )

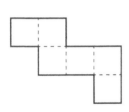

d. (   )

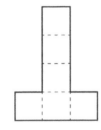

e. (   )

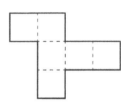

f. (   )

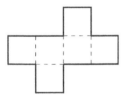

g. (   )

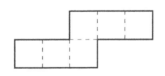

h. (   )

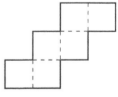

i. (   )

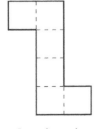

j. (   )

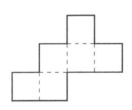

k. (   )

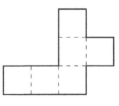

l. (   )

2. Write a tick (✓) in the brackets for each net that can be folded to form a cuboid.

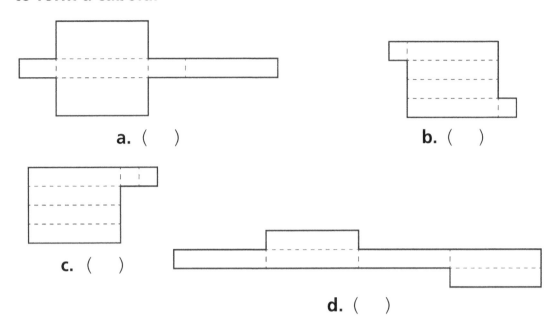

a. (   )

b. (   )

c. (   )

d. (   )

1. This diagram shows the net of a cube. Think carefully, then fill in the brackets.

No. 1 face is opposite No. (   ) face.

No. 2 face is opposite No. (   ) face.

No. 3 face is opposite No. (   ) face.

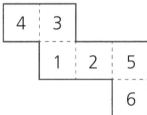

2. This diagram shows the net of a cuboid. Think carefully, then fill in the brackets.

We can use the measurements marked on the diagram to work out the volume of the cuboid: (   ) cubic centimetres (units: cm)

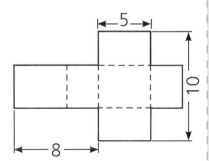

7. Surface areas of cuboids and cubes

Pupil Textbook page 58–61

1. Multiple choice – write the letter of the correct answer in the brackets.

a. Which of the following nets cannot be folded to form a cube? ( )

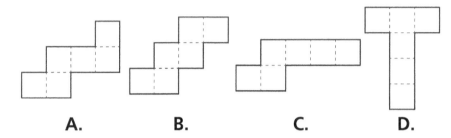

| A. | B. | C. | D. |

b. The edge of a cube is 6 cm. What is the surface area? ( )

    A. 72 cm²   **B.** 36 cm²   **C.** 216 cm²   **D.** 216 cm³

c. The edge of a cube is 6 cm. Compare its volume with its surface area. ( )

    A. The same.   **B.** The volume is bigger.

    C. The surface area is bigger.   **D.** Cannot be compared.

d. If the edge of a cube increases by 2 times, the surface area increases ( ) times.

    A. 2   **B.** 4   **C.** 6   **D.** 8

2. Work out the surface area of each cube.

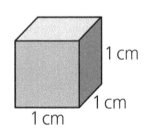

1 cm
1 cm
1 cm

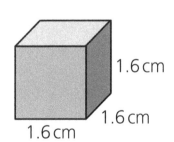

1.6 cm
1.6 cm
1.6 cm

3. The surface area of a cube is 48 square metres. What is the area of one face?

4. To make a cube-shaped paper box without a lid, which has edges of 4 cm, at least how many square centimetres of paper are needed?

Level **B**

1. If the sum of the edges of a cube is 48 cm, what is its surface area?

2. Alex built a cube with an edge of 4 centimetres with some centimetre cubes and coloured its surface.

    a. There are (   ) centimetre cubes with 3 coloured faces.

    b. There are (   ) centimetre cubes with 2 coloured faces.

    c. There are (   ) centimetre cubes with 1 coloured face.

    d. There are (   ) centimetre cubes with no coloured faces.

1. Fill in the brackets.

a. The surface area of a cube or a cuboid is the (   ) of the areas of its (   ).

b. If the cuboid shown in the diagram below is a cm long, b cm wide and h cm high, the areas of its top and bottom faces are both (   ) square centimetres and the areas of its front and back faces are both (   ) square centimetres.

c. If a cuboid is 5 cm long, 4 cm wide and 3 cm high, its surface area is (   ) square centimetres.

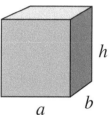

2. Complete the tables by filling in the blanks.

Cuboid	length	4 cm	8 m
	width	2 cm	8 m
	height	0.5 cm	6 m
	surface area		

Cube	length of edge	0.5 m	7 cm	10 cm
	surface area			

3. Dylan wants to make a paper box with a lid. It will be 6 cm long, 2 cm wide and 4 cm high. Help him to work out the smallest number of square centimetres of paper he needs.

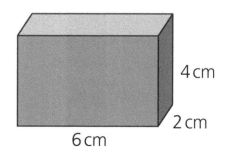

4 cm

2 cm

6 cm

4. Emma's father paints the surface of a cuboid block of wood, which is 25 cm long, 10 cm wide and 5 cm high. What is the area of the painted surface?

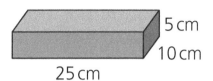

5 cm
10 cm
25 cm

Level **B**

1. A room (with a flat ceiling) is 6 m long, 3.3 m wide and 3 m high. The total area of the doors and windows is 8 square metres. Matt is painting the walls and the ceiling. What area, in square metres, will he paint? If it takes 0.4 kg of paint to cover 1 square metre, how many kilograms of paint will he need?

2. The top diagram is the back face and the bottom diagram is the top face of a cuboid. The area of the back face is (   ) square centimetres, and the surface area of the cuboid is (   ) square centimetres.

10 cm

| Back face | 5 cm |

10 cm

| Top face | 7 cm |

8. Practice exercise

Pupil Textbook page 62 Level **A**

1. A construction team is building a cuboid structure from wooden panels. The structure is 8 m long, 5 m wide and 6 m high. The long front face is the last piece to go on. The area of this piece is ( ) square metres.

2. A cuboid is 5 cm long, 3 cm wide and 2 cm high. The total length of its edges is ( ) cm, its surface area is ( ) cm² and its volume is ( ) cm³.

3. Emma's room is 4.2 m long, 3.5 m wide, 3 m high and the total area of its windows and doors is 4.5 m². If the walls in the room are all covered in wallpaper, at least how many square metres of wallpaper will be used?

4. Find the volume of the combined 3D shape. (units: m)

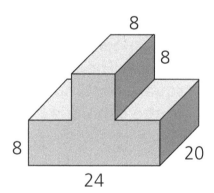

5. The surface area of a cube is 600 cm², so its volume is (   ) cm³.

6. A cuboid is 10 cm high, and its bottom face is square with a 32 cm perimeter. The surface area of the cuboid is (   ) cm².

Level **B**

1. A small cuboid was cut from the corner of a cube. The surfaces of the new shape were painted. What is the area of the painted faces? (units: cm)

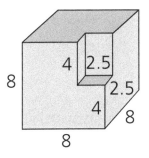

2. A cuboid gift box, 10 cm long, 15 cm wide and 8 cm high, is wrapped with a silk ribbon and a knot is tied, using a further 40 cm of the silk ribbon. What is the total length of ribbon needed to wrap the whole gift box?

9. Changes in surface area

Pupil Textbook pages 63–67

1. **Multiple choice – write the letter of the correct answer in the brackets.**

   a. As shown, a cuboid wooden rod is cut into 4 pieces. There are ( ) more faces than before.

   A. 3   **B.** 4
   C. 6   **D.** 8

   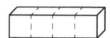

   b. If we build a cuboid with three cubes with sides of 2 centimetres, the surface area of the built cuboid is ( ) square centimetres smaller than the sum of the surface areas of the three cubes.

   A. 24   **B.** 16   **C.** 12   **D.** 6

2. **As shown, six centimetre cubes can be arranged to form two cuboids, A and B. Which cuboid has the larger surface area?**

   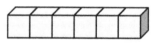

   A B

3. **As shown, a cuboid that is 3.6 cm long can be cut into 3 identical cubes. How much greater is the sum of the surface areas of the three cubes than the surface area of the cuboid?**

   3.6 cm

4. **As shown, a cube with edges 1 cm long is cut from the corner of a larger cube, which has an edge length of 10 cm. What is the volume of the remaining 3D shape? What is the change in the surface area?**

   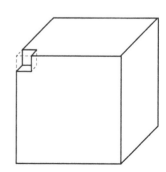

5. How many possibilities are there if two identical cuboids, as shown in the diagram, are used to form a larger cuboid? What is the surface area of each possibility? (Use a drawing to help you understand the problem.)

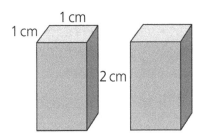

1 cm
1 cm
2 cm

1. As shown, a cube with a surface area of 516 cm² is cut into 8 identical cubes (all of the large cube is used). How much greater is the sum of the surface areas of the 8 cubes than the surface area of the large cube?

2. Multiple choice – write the letter of the correct answer in the brackets.

a. Alex uses five identical cubes to form a 3D shape. The shape with the smallest surface area is (   ).

      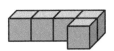   

   A.   **B.**   **C.**   **D.**

b. Which of these 3D shapes has a different surface area to the others? (   )

   A.   **B.**   **C.**   **D.**

10. Volume and capacity

Pupil Textbook pages 68–71

1. Fill in the brackets.

3.02 l = (   ) cm³   456 ml = (   ) cm³

1203 cm³ = (   ) l 0.01 m³ = (   ) ml

0.05 l = (   ) cm³   320 ml = (   ) cm³

0.45 l = (   ) cm³

2100 ml = (   ) cm³

2. The level of water in a measuring cup is at 700 ml on the scale. It rises to 900 ml after some stones are immersed in it. This means that the volume of the stones is (   ).

3. As shown, a cuboid-shaped pool is 8 m long, 6.5 m wide and 5 m deep. If it is filled with water, how many cubic metres of water will it hold?

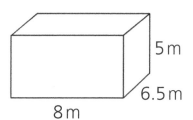

5 m

6.5 m

8 m

4. An empty, cube-shaped fuel tank is 25 cm long on its inside edge. How many litres of fuel can the tank hold? As shown, how many litres of fuel will have been poured in to give a depth of 8 cm?

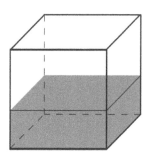

5. A cuboid-shaped swimming pool is 50 m long, 21 m wide and 2.5 m deep. Water flows into the pool to a depth of 1.8 m. How much will this cost if the price is £1.92 for 1 cubic metre of water?

1. A cuboid-shaped tank is filled with water. Then a cuboid stone, which is 10 cm in both height and width, is put into it, and 4 litres of water spill out of the tank. What is the length of the stone?

2. An open-topped iron cuboid box is 26 cm long and 16 cm wide. The four corners are cut from its base, to give shapes with three square faces, of side 3 cm. These are welded to form a square iron box without a cover. What is the capacity of the new iron box?

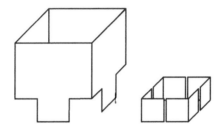

3. The water in two containers, A and B, has the same height but the area of the base of B is 2 times that of A. If identical solid iron blocks are immersed in both containers, the height of water rises higher in container (   ). If the height of water increases by 4 cm in container A, the height in B will increase by (   ) cm.

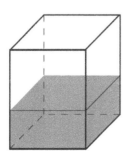

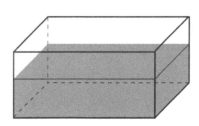

A B

11. Volume and mass

Pupil Textbook page 72

Level **A**

1. On a construction site, exactly 441 tonnes of sand are poured into a cuboid sandpit 14 m long, 10.5 m wide and 2 m deep. What is the mass of 1 cubic metre of sand?

2. A plastic bottle can hold 2.8 kg of vegetable oil at most. How many litres can the bottle contain if each litre weighs 0.8 kg?

Level **B**

1. A cuboid-shaped fuel tank is 0.9 m long, 0.6 m wide and 0.5 m high. It is full of unleaded petrol. What is the mass of the tank of petrol, if the petrol weighs 0.73 kg per litre?

2. An iron block that weighs 11.7 kg is put into a cuboid glass water tank, which is 50 cm long, 30 cm wide and 25 cm high. How many centimetres will the water rise if the iron block is immersed in the water and none spills out? (The iron block weighs 7800 kg per cubic metre.)

Unit Five: Probability

Each team has five players. If every player shakes hands with all the players in the opposing team, how many handshakes are there in total?

The table below lists the sections in this unit.

After completing each section, assess your work. (Use 😃 if you are satisfied with your progress or 😐 if you are not satisfied.)

Section	Self-assessment
1. Probability	
2. Evaluate probability	
3. Number of possible events	

1. Probability

Pupil Textbook pages 74–75

1. Fill in the brackets.

 a. An event that is (   ) will definitely happen .

 b. When it is not certain that an event will happen, it is a (   ) event.

 c. An event that definitely cannot happen is (   ).

2. What happens for certain in the following events? What can't happen? What can happen? Put a tick in the appropriate box.

Event	Must happen	Impossible	May happen
The coin faces up as it drops to the ground.			
It will rain tomorrow after school.			
Jill goes to Grandma's house on 31 February.			
Monday will follow Sunday.			

3. A computer screen is constantly scrolling (with the same time intervals) to show the numbers from 1 to 9. Fill in 'possible', 'impossible' or 'certain'.

 a. Pause the screen, and it shows one of the 9 numbers: (   )

 b. Pause the screen, and the number is 0: (   )

 c. Pause the screen twice, and the sum of the two numbers is 7: (   )

4. One ball is taken from each of the boxes below. What is the result? Match each box to a description.

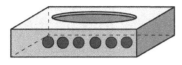 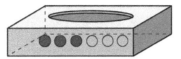 

| 6 red balls | 3 red balls plus 3 green balls | 6 green balls |

| It must be a green ball. | Maybe it's a green ball. | It can't be a green ball. |

5. Multiple choice – write the letter of the correct answer in the brackets.

a. It is (   ) that a negative number is less than a natural number.

   A. possible   **B.** certain   **C.** impossible

b. It is (   ) that an equilateral triangle can be an isosceles triangle, but it is (   ) that an isosceles triangle can be an equilateral triangle.

   A. possible   **B.** certain   **C.** impossible

6. There are 9 balls of the same size, marked 1–9. Choose four of the numbers to go into each box to set up the following conditions. (Write the numbers on the balls.)

a. Pick a ball, and it is certain that the number will be even.

b. Pick a ball, and it is possible that the number will be even.

c. Pick a ball, and an even number is impossible.

1. Put 9 small squares into 3 boxes, with every box having one square at least; the number of squares in each box is not the same. (Write the number of squares in every box in the table.)

	Box 1	Box 2	Box 3
Arrangement 1			
Arrangement 2			
Arrangement 3			

(Note: 2, 3, 4 and 2, 4, 3 in each box is the same arrangement.)

2. Is it possible to put 20 small squares into 6 boxes, with every box having one square at least? The number of squares in each box is not the same. Have a try.

2. Evaluate probability

Pupil Textbook pages 76–77

1. Multiple choice – write the letter of the correct answer in the brackets.

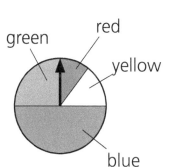

a. The pointer on the wheel spins. When the pointer stops it is most probable that it will point to the (   ) area.

A. blue   **B.** green

C. red   **D.** yellow

b. There are 7 red balls, 5 yellow balls, 2 blue balls and 5 green balls in one bag. They are identical apart from the colour. Pick a ball at random. The colour that has the maximum probability of being picked is (   ). The colour that has the minimum probability of being picked is (   ). The (   ) and (   ) balls both have the same probability.

A. blue   **B.** green   **C.** red   **D.** yellow

2. A and B play some games, but is the rule of each game fair? (Put a '✓' in the brackets if it is fair, and a 'X' in the brackets if it is unfair.)

a. Toss a coin such that A will win if the coin is face up, and B will win if the coin is face down.   (   )

b. Roll a dice. A will win if the number is greater than 3, and B will win if the number is less than 3.   (   )

c. Play rock–paper–scissors.   (   )

3. There are nine cards, marked 1–9.

Choose six cards to play a game with the following conditions. (Write the numbers on the cards.)

a. Choose one card with the same probability of being even or odd.

b. Choose one card with a greater probability of being even than of being odd.

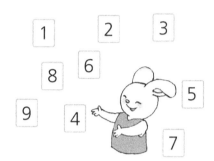

c. Choose one card with a greater probability of being odd than of being even.

4. Fill in the brackets.

a. A box contains 20 balls that are coloured red or yellow. Dylan randomly picks a ball. If the probability of picking a red ball is less than that of picking a yellow ball, there are (   ) red balls at most.

b. A box contains 25 balls that are coloured red or yellow. Dylan randomly picks a ball. If the probability of picking a red ball is greater than that of picking a yellow ball, there are (   ) red balls at least.

Dylan and Poppy play a game with two identical coins. They toss their coins at the same time. Look at the rules below to decide if they are fair. Write who will have the greater probability of winning.

a. If the two coins land with both heads or both tails up, Dylan wins, and if the two coins land with different faces up, Poppy wins.
(   )

b. If the two coins both land with heads up, Dylan wins, and if the two coins both land with tails up, Poppy wins. (   )

c. If the two coins have the same face up, Dylan wins, but for any other result, Poppy wins. (   )

3. Number of possible events

Pupil Textbook pages 78–82

1. A box contains four digit cards: 3, 5, 7 and 8.

How many different two-digit numbers can you make by picking two cards from the box?

a. Complete the tree diagram and fill in the numbers in the brackets.

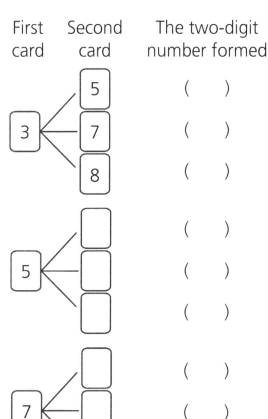

First card	Second card	The two-digit number formed
3	5	( )
	7	( )
	8	( )
5		( )
		( )
		( )
7		( )
		( )
		( )
8		( )
		( )
		( )

b. Complete the table.

Second card / First card	3	5	7	8
3				
5				
7				
8				

c. From the tree diagram and the table, we can use four cards to form (   ) different two-digit numbers.

2. Fill in the brackets.

    a. The supermarket sells cola, lemonade, orange juice, apple juice and milk. Dylan wants to pick two drinks. He has (   ) ways of choosing.

    b. There are six people in Alex's group. There are (   ) choices to select one group leader and one vice group leader.

    c. Two teams have a match, and each team has five players. If every player shakes hands with all the players in the other team, there are (   ) handshakes in all.

3. Today the school dinner menu has four meat dishes, three vegetable dishes and two soups.

    a. To choose one meat dish and one vegetable dish, there are (   ) choices.

    b. To choose one meat dish and one soup, there are (   ) choices.

    c. To choose one meat dish, one vegetable dish and one soup, there are (   ) choices.

Roll one red and one yellow dice. Complete the table with all possible sums of the two numbers.

Yellow Red	1	2	3	4	5	6
1	2	3	4	5	6	7
2						
3						
4						
5						
6						

a. There are ( ) with the sum = 2.
There are ( ) with the sum = 3.
There are ( ) with the sum = 4.
There are ( ) with the sum = 5.
There are ( ) with the sum = 6.
There are ( ) with the sum = 7.
There are ( ) with the sum = 8.
There are ( ) with the sum = 9.
There are ( ) with the sum = 10.
There are ( ) with the sum = 11.
There are ( ) with the sum = 12.

b. There are ( ) sums that are a multiple of 3.

c. Dylan and Emma agree that Emma will win if the sum = 5, 6, 7 or 8, and Dylan will win with all other results. Do you think it is fair? ( ) Fill in 'fair' or 'unfair', and write your reason.

Unit Six: Consolidating and enhancing

What is the average number of private cars per year over these 7 years?

The numbers of privately owned cars in Shanghai from 2006 to 2012 was (in thousands) 409, 502, 597, 711, 865, 989 and 1146, respectively.

The table below lists the sections in this unit.

After completing each section, assess your work. (Use 😊 if you are satisfied with your progress or 😐 if you are not satisfied.)

Section	Self-assessment
1. Number operations	
2. Equations and algebra	
3. Shape and geometry	
4. Basic statistics	

1. Number operations

Pupil Textbook pages 84–93

Level **A**

1. Fill in the brackets.

a. The diameter of the Sun is 1 392 000 km. Using millions as a unit, this is written as ( ) million kilometres.

b. Eighty plus zero point zero eight can be written as ( ). 100.07 can be read as ( ).

c. The decimal number that consists of 9 ones, 4 hundredths and 3 thousandths is ( ).

d. There are ( ) 0.001 units in 0.8. The decimal number of 280 units of 0.001 can be simplified as ( ).

e. If we order 1.414, 1.441, 4.141 and 4.114 from greatest to smallest, the third number is ( ).

f. The shaded part of the diagram is ( ) of the whole area.

g. Fill in the boxes with the appropriate decimal numbers.

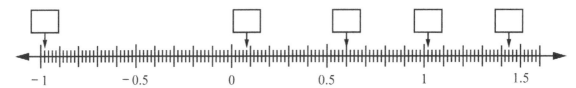

h. Fill in each ◯ with the appropriate fraction, and each ☐ with the appropriate decimal number.

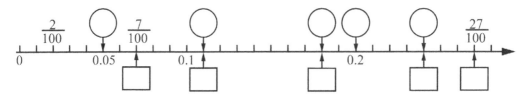

i. Rounding 3.2817 to the nearest whole number gives ( ), and is different from the original number by ( ).

j. An apple has a mass of 240 grams. (   ) of these apples have a mass of 6 kilograms in total.

k. Alex uses £4 to buy pencils, which are 36p each. He can buy (   ) pencils at most, and has £(   ) left.

2. Unit conversion

$125\,ml = ($ $)\,l$ $0.08\,t = ($ $)\,kg$

$620\,cm^3 = ($ $)\,ml$ $2.36\,m^2 = ($ $)\,cm^2$

$42.195\,km = ($ $)\,m$ $2.07\,cm^3 = ($ $)\,l$

3 minutes 12 seconds = (   ) seconds $13.6\,g = ($ $)\,kg$

3. Write the results quickly.

$3.7 + 7.3 =$ $0.56 - 0.44 =$

$1.6 \times 0.5 =$ $1 \div 0.25 =$

$6.25 \times 4 =$ $0.01 \div 0.2 =$

$2.4 \times 5 =$ $3.256 \div 0.8 =$

$1 + 0.8 - 1 + 0.8 =$ $0.4 - 0.4 \times 0.4 =$

$5.5 \times 0.8 \div 1.1 =$ $(2.5 + 0.75) \div 0.25 =$

$\dfrac{4}{7} + \dfrac{3}{7} =$ $\dfrac{590}{1000} - \dfrac{490}{1000} =$

$\dfrac{9}{10} - \dfrac{28}{100} =$ $\dfrac{11}{18} + \dfrac{7}{18} - \dfrac{5}{18} =$

4. Use the column method and check the answers.

$320.4 - 10.95 =$ $8.67 + 10.48 =$

$0.75 \times 5.6 =$ $2.904 \div 0.48 =$

5. How can you work out 18 × 15? Fill in the brackets and have a try.

18 × 15
= 18 × (   ) + 18 × (   )
=
=

18 × 15
= 20 × (   ) − 2 × (   )
=
=

18 × 15
= 2 × 15 × (   )
=
=

Do you have any other methods to work it out? Have a try.

6. Work these out, showing the steps in your calculation. Simplify as much as possible.

14.3 + 1.82 + 0.8

32.26 − 14.46 − 5.64

0.25 × 28

4.8 ÷ 1.25

24.4 × 7.5 ÷ 6.1

12.5 × (8 + 0.8)

5.6 × 4.4 + 4.4 × 3.4 + 4.4

[17.45 − (7.45 + 4.75) × 0.25] ÷ 0.24

7. True or false? Put a tick (✓) for 'true' or a cross (✗) for 'false' in the brackets.

    a. 0.3 represents 3 hundredths.   ( )

    b. There are 204 units of 0.01 in 2.04.   ( )

    c. $a \div 0.01 = a \times 100$ ( )

    d. The sum of five two-digit numbers will be no more than 495.   ( )

    e. If we rewrite 3.45 as a new number without the decimal point, the new number is 100 times greater than the original number.   ( )

8. Write the equations and work them out.

    a. Find the difference of the quotient of 9 divided by 0.6 and the product of 9 multiplied by 0.6.

    b. Multiply 2 lots of 0.8 and divide the product by the sum of 2 lots of 0.8. What is the quotient?

9. Multiple choice – write the letter of the correct answer in the brackets.

    a. $8.5 > \square > 8.4$

        ( ) two-digit decimal numbers can be written in the $\square$.

        A. 0   **B.** 9   **C.** Countless   **D.** 100

    b. Of the four numbers 1.2, 0.5, 0.9 and $\frac{7}{10}$, the smallest number is ( ).

        A. 1.2   **B.** 0.5   **C.** 0.9   **D.** $\frac{7}{10}$

    c. We know that $M > 0$, so the incorrect relationship is ( ).

        A. $M \div 0.1 > M$ **B.** $M \times 1.1 > M$

        C. $M \times 0.999 < M$ **D.** $M \div 1.01 > M$

d. When a three-digit decimal number is rounded to two decimal places, the result is 8.60. The original number must be (   ).

 A. more than or equal to 8.59, but less than 8.64

 B. more than or equal to 8.595, but less than 8.604

 C. more than or equal to 8.60, but less than 8.64

 D. more than or equal to 8.595, but less than 8.605

10. Read each question carefully and work out the answer.

 a. If 24 litres of juice are poured into 1.25 litre bottles, how many bottles can be filled? How much is left over?

 b. A bus and a truck start from opposite ends of a motorway between two cities at the same time and travel towards each other. The speed of the bus is 102 kilometres per hour and the speed of the truck is 81 kilometres per hour. After 1.5 hours, they meet. What is the distance between the two cities?

 c. A family are driving from central Shanghai to the countryside for a day out. The total volume of their car's fuel tank is 60 litres. If the car uses super unleaded petrol, how much will they need to spend (in Chinese yuan) to fill up the tank if there are 12 litres left in it?

Type of fuel	Price (yuan per litre)
super unleaded	7.45
unleaded	7.85
diesel	7.01

d. A car travels 60 kilometres in 0.75 hours. At this speed, how long does it take to travel 40 kilometres?

e. The school PE teacher takes £200 to the sports shop. He buys 4 basketballs first and uses the money left to buy footballs. How many footballs can he buy?

£14.60   £11.80

f. There are 15 footballs in the PE room, which is 3 times more than the number of basketballs. The number of volleyballs is three less than twice the number of basketballs. How many volleyballs are there in the PE room?

g. A supermarket orders 600 kilograms of apples and a quantity of pears. The apples fill 4 fewer boxes than the pears fill. Each box of apples weighs 25 kilograms, and each box of pears weighs 22 kilograms. What is the total mass of the pears?

1. Use a shortcut strategy to calculate these quickly.

$(5.3 \times 3.75 + 3.75 \times 3.5) \div 2.2$ $9.6 \div (4.8 \times 7.2 + 2.8 \times 4.8)$

2. a. Write 3.69, 3.6̇9̇6̇, 3.6969, 3.96, 3.9̇6̇ in order from greatest to
smallest on the line below.

_____

b. The rules of a game are explained in the flowchart.
If the number input is 100, then the last number displayed is
(   ).

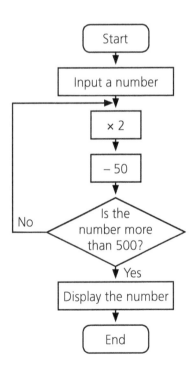

Start

Input a number

× 2

− 50

Is the number more than 500?

No

Yes

Display the number

End

c. The time displayed on a digital clock is 13:11. There are (   )
until the same number is next displayed on the digital clock.

d. When Dylan was working out the addition of decimal numbers,
he was careless and didn't notice that for one number he had
'3' instead of '8' in the tens place, and '9' instead of '6' in
the tenths place. Dylan's result was 93.2. The correct answer
is (   ).

e. I have a three-digit number. If I rewrite my number with a
decimal point in it, it will be 101.7 less than my original number.
My original three-digit number is (   ).

2. Equations and algebra

Pupil Textbook pages 94–98　　　　　　　　　Level **A**

1. **Fill in each ☐ with the appropriate number or letter. Fill in each circle with the appropriate operation symbol.**

   a. $140 - 25 - 75$
      $= 140 - (25 + 75)$

      $1200 - 37 - 163$
      $= 1200 - (\boxed{} + \boxed{})$

      Generally, $a - b - c = \boxed{} \bigcirc (\boxed{} \bigcirc \boxed{})$

   b. $120 \div 25 \div 75$
      $= 120 \div (25 \times 75)$

      $38\,000 \div 125 \div 8$
      $= 38\,000 \div (\boxed{} \times \boxed{})$

      Generally, $a \div b \div c = \boxed{} \bigcirc (\boxed{} \bigcirc \boxed{})$

      (b and c are not equal to 0.)

2. **Fill in the brackets.**

   a. A company has to move a tonnes of goods. It has a truck that can carry b tonnes. After the truck has made 3 trips, there are (　　　) tonnes of goods left to move.

   b. A car travels at a kilometres per hour on average, and a truck travels at b kilometres per hour on average ($a > b$). The car and truck both travel s kilometres, so the car takes (　　) fewer hours than the truck.

   c. Write an equation that shows the quantity relationship in the diagram.

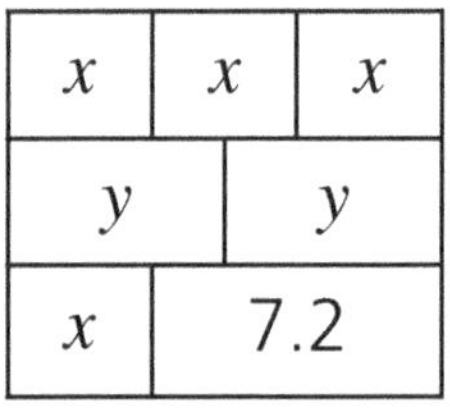

      (　　　　　　　　　　)

x	x	x
y		y
x		7.2

      We can work out from the diagram that
      $x = ($　　$), y = ($　　$).$

   d. You are given a start number. Double it and add 1 to the result, then divide the result by 4 to give the final number.

      If the start number is 4.5, then the final number is (　　).

      If the final number is 4.5, then the start number is (　　).

3. Multiple choice – write the letter of the correct answer in the brackets.

a. If $a = bx + c$, then of the equations below, ( ) is also true.

A. $c = bx - a$ **B.** $a + c = bx$

C. $c = a - bx$ **D.** $bx - c = a$

b. A is twice B, and B is three times C. If C is x, then the sum of A, B and C is ( ).

A. $5x$ **B.** $6x$ **C.** $9x$ **D.** $10x$

4. Find the value.

a. When $a = 178$ and $b = 53$, find the value of $48a - 48b$.

b. When $a = 2.6$ and $b = 1.3$, find the value of $a^2 - 1.3b$.

5. Solve the equations.

a. $5x \div 2 = 7$ b. $8x - 0.4 \times 6 = 0$ c. $6x + 9 = 2.4 \times 5$

d. $0.5 (x - 3) = 31.5$ e. $2.2x - x = 4.2 \div 2$ f. $x + 5.6 = 3x$

6. Write the equations and find the results.

a. 5 times A is 3 times B. Given that A is 6.6, find B.

b. 3 times a number is 1.8 times more than the number itself. What is the number?

7. Write equations to solve the problems.

a. There are 48 flowers. If they are tied into bunches of 5, and there are 3 flowers left over, how many bunches are there?

b. A fruit farm harvests 600 kilograms of pears and oranges in total. If the mass of the pears is 1.5 times more than the oranges, then what are the masses of the pears and of the oranges?

c. A farm fruit shop has apples and pears for sale. The mass of the apples is 1.5 times more than the mass of the pears. After selling 60 kilograms of apples but no pears, the masses of apples and pears are equal. What were the masses of apples and of pears to start with?

d. There are 21 footballs in the PE room. The number of basketballs is 3 times more than the number of footballs plus 8, and twice the number of volleyballs minus 5. How many basketballs and how many volleyballs are there?

e. A trapezium has a height of 5 centimetres, with a bottom base 1.8 times more than the top base. If 4.8 centimetres is added to the length of the top base, and the bottom base and height remain the same, the trapezium will become a parallelogram.

   i. What is the length of the trapezium's top base, in centimetres?

   ii. Find the area of the trapezium.

f. The perimeter of parallelogram *ABCD* is 80 cm, *BC* = 24 cm and *AE* = 12 cm.

i. Find the length of *AB*.

ii. Find the length of *AF*.

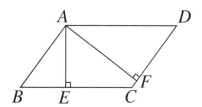

g. The distance between two cities is 450 kilometres. Two cars set out, one from each city, at the same time and travel towards each other. The first car travels at 85 km/h, on average, and the second car at 95 km/h, on average. How many hours is it before they meet?

h. Two cars, A and B, start at the same time from two places 300 kilometres apart and travel towards each other. After 2.5 hours, they meet. Car A travels 10 kilometres more than car B. Find the speed of the two cars.

i. Emma leaves the school and Dylan leaves the swimming pool at the same time. They walk towards each other along the same road. They meet on the road exactly half way between the school and the swimming pool. Read their conversation, below, and work out how many minutes Emma had been walking from the start to when they met. What is the distance, in metres, between the school and the swimming pool?

I start 5 minutes later than Emma, at 80 metres per minute.

I walk from the school to the swimming pool at 60 metres per minute.

j. Some new books have arrived in the library and they are going to be distributed evenly on several new bookshelves. If 40 books are put on each bookshelf, 15 books are left over. If 45 books are put on each bookshelf, no books are left over. How many new bookshelves are there? How many new books are there in total?

k. Dylan's mother bought equal numbers of pears and apples. Dylan's family eats 2 pears and 5 apples every day. When they had eaten all the apples, 12 pears were left. How many days did the apples last? How many pears and how many apples did Dylan's mother buy in total?

l. Two vans, A and B, both carrying vegetables, set out from a fruit and vegetable farm and drive along the same road to a farmers' market. During the trip, van A breaks down and is delayed for 0.2 hours. The two vans finally arrive at the farmers' market at the same time, 2 hours after they left the farm. Given that van A travels at 65 km/h, on average, what is the speed of van B, in km/h, on average?

1 Fill in the brackets.

  a. If $5 \times 3 + a = 8 \times 30 - b$, the value of $a + b$ is (   ).

  b. If $a \times 0.25 = b \div 0.25 = 8$, a is (   ) times more than b.

2. Look at the line segment diagram. The incorrect equation is (   ).

  A. $20 + 35 - x = 48$

  B. $48 - 35 = 20 - x$

  C. $20 + x + 35 = 48$

  D. $48 + x = 35 + 20$

3. Write equations to solve the problems.

  a. Oliver walks to school from home in the morning. If he walks at 60 metres per minute, he will be 4 minutes late. If he walks at 75 metres per minute, he'll arrive at school on time. One day, Oliver sets off from home in the morning and walks at 80 metres per minute. Will he arrive at school in 12 minutes?

  b. There are two ships, A and B. Ship A sails at a constant speed of 24 kilometres per hour, and ship B sails at a constant speed of 16 kilometres per hour. They start at the same time from the same place and travel in opposite directions. Two hours later, ship A changes direction to chase ship B because of a problem. After how many hours will ship A catch up with ship B?

3. Shapes and geometry

Pupil Textbook pages 99–110

Level **A**

1. True or false? Put a tick (✓) for 'true' or a cross (✗) for 'false' in the brackets.

   a. If one of the angles of two lines that intersect is a right angle, then the other three angles must be right angles.　( )

   b. The area of a triangle is half the area of a parallelogram with the same base and height.　( )

   c. A triangle can't be both an acute triangle and an isosceles triangle. ( )

   d. The perpendicular distance between two parallel lines is equal at every point.　( )

   e. A right-angled triangle only has one height.　( )

   f. We can use a ruler to measure the length of half a line segment. ( )

   g. A circle is a symmetrical shape, and it has a line of symmetry.　( )

   h. Quadrilaterals with two pairs of parallel sides may be rectangles. ( )

   i. In a cuboid, three edges meet at a point and they are all perpendicular to each other.　( )

   j. If the two faces of a cuboid are rectangular, then it is a cube.　( )

2. Multiple choice – write the letter of the correct answer in the brackets.

   a. Shape ( ) is not the net of a cube.

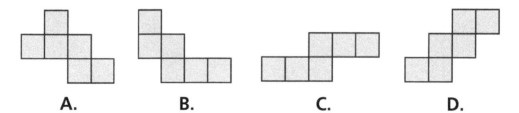

   A.　　　　　　B.　　　　　　C.　　　　　　D.

   b. Alex uses a pair of set squares to make angles of different sizes by placing them together. The smallest obtuse angle he can make is ( ) degrees.

   A. 135　　**B.** 120　　**C.** 105　　**D.** 75

3. Draw the other half of each shape so that it is symmetrical, with AB as the line of symmetry.

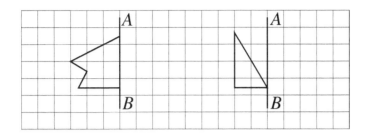

4. Find the area of each shape. (units: cm)

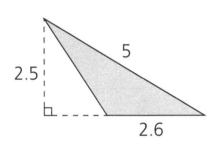

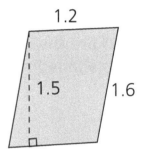

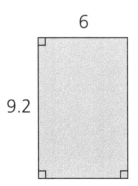

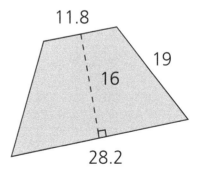

5. Find the area of each of these compound shapes. (units: cm)

a.

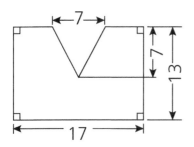

b.

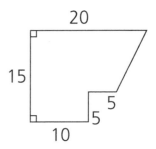

6. In the diagram, the area of rectangle $ABCD$ is 96 cm², and E, F and G are the midpoints of AD, BC and CD. Work out the area of the shaded region.

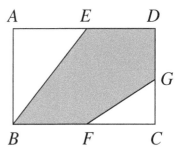

7. Find the surface areas and volumes of the cuboid and the cube. (units: m)

a.

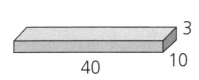

b.

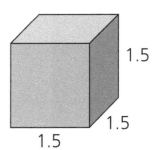

8. The volume of the letter 'E' in the diagram is
(   ) cm³. (units: cm)

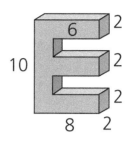

9. A shape is made up of four right-angled triangles of the same size. The base of each triangle is 40 cm, and the height is 30 cm.

    a. What is the area of the whole shape, in square metres?

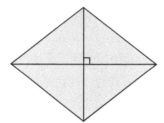

    b. If we paint both sides of the whole shape and use 550 m*l* of paint for each square metre, how many litres of paint do we need?

10. Dylan draws the side view of a staircase (see diagram). What is the perimeter of Dylan's shape?

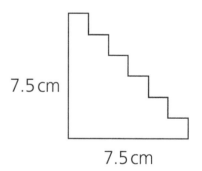

11. The school built a cuboid-shaped swimming pool that was 50 metres long, 20 metres wide and 2.5 metres deep.

    a. How many square metres of tiles will be needed to cover the walls and the base of the swimming pool?

    b. The depth of the water in the pool is 2 metres. How many cubic metres of water are there in the pool?

1. Fill in the brackets.

a. A rectangle is 24 cm long and 16 cm wide. A square can be joined to it to make a large rectangle. The area of the large rectangle is (   ) cm² or (   ) cm².

b. A large cuboid is made by joining three cubes of the same size. If the total length of the edges is reduced by 48 cm, the surface area is reduced by (   ) cm².

2. Multiple choice – write the letter of the correct answer in the brackets.

a. The perimeter of a rectangle is 24 centimetres. If both the length and width increase by 3 cm, its area increases by (   ) square centimetres.

    A. 9   **B.** 36   **C.** 45   **D.** 72

b. The top and bottom faces of a cuboid are rectangles, with length 5 cm and width 4 cm. The other two faces are squares, so the surface area of the cuboid is at least (   ) square centimetres.

    A. 76   **B.** 96   **C.** 112   **D.** 130

3. The diagram shows a 3-polyomino, which is a shape made from three equal squares. We can add another square to the 3-polyomino to make a 4-polyomino.
Add squares to the shapes below to make four different 4-polyominos. Given that the sides of each small square are 1 cm long, work out the perimeter of each your 4-polyominoes.

1 cm

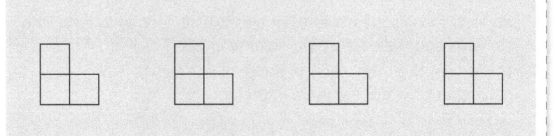

4. Basic statistics

Pupil Textbook pages 111–114

1. Fill in the brackets.

  a. A school counts the number of pupils in each year. A (   ) graph is the best way to display the information.

  b. The best way to show increases and decreases of a quantity clearly is in a (   ) graph.

  c. A British women's volleyball team has a friendly game with a German women's volleyball team. At the beginning of the game, each team has 6 players on the court. If each player shakes hands with all the players on the other team, then they shake hands (   ) times in all.

  d. There are 4 people in Alex's group, and they are playing a game called 'calculating 24 points'. If every pair plays a game, then they have to play ( ) times.

  e. If the average of the 3 numbers, A, B and C is a, and the average of A and B is b, then the number C is (   ). (Express it in terms of a and b.)

2. Multiple choice – write the letter of the correct answer in the brackets.

It is known that the masses of four pupils, a, b, c and d, are 40 kg, 44 kg, 48 kg and 50 kg, respectively. Estimate the average mass of the four pupils. ( )

  A. Below 40 kg   **B.** Between 40 kg and 45 kg

  C. Between 45 kg and 50 kg   **D.** More than 50 kg

3. Read each question carefully and work out the answer.

a. Alex walked from one end of the school hall to the other four times and took, respectively, 64 steps, 62 steps, 63 steps and 65 steps. If the distance he covers in 10 steps is 5.2 metres, estimate the length of the hall. (Round to the nearest whole number.)

b. The table on the right gives information about the families in a block of flats.

2 people per household	14 households
3 people per household	19 households
4 people per household	7 households

   i. In this building, there are (   ) people in each flat, on average.

   ii. Estimating in this way, if there are 10 similar buildings in the neighbourhood, the number of residents is about (   ).

   iii. The neighbourhood committee is going to make a key card for each resident. The price for each card is £20. The total cost will be about £(   ).

c. The chart shows the average daily temperature in London from 25 to 31 March.

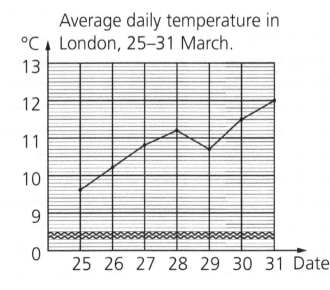

Average daily temperature in London, 25–31 March.

Country lore – the start of spring
If the average daily temperature on 5 consecutive days is greater than or equal to 10 °C, then the first of the 5 days is the start of spring.

i. If springtime is judged according to the chart, in the year shown spring starts on ___ (day) ___ (month).

ii. In the week shown, the average temperature is about ___ °C. (Round the answer to the nearest whole number.)

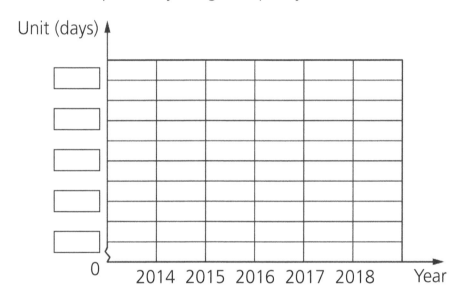

1. The table below shows the number of days of good quality air in Manchester each year over a period of five years. Use this data to make a line graph.

Table of days of good quality air in Manchester

Year	2014	2015	2016	2017	2018
Number of days	328	334	336	337	343

Graph of days of good quality air in Manchester

Unit (days)

0   2014 2015 2016 2017 2018   Year

2. The table below shows the numbers of privately owned cars in Shanghai from 2006 to 2012. Use the data to make a line graph and fill in the blanks to answer the questions.

Year	2006	2007	2008	2009	2010	2011	2012
Cars (thousands)	409	502	597	711	865	989	1146

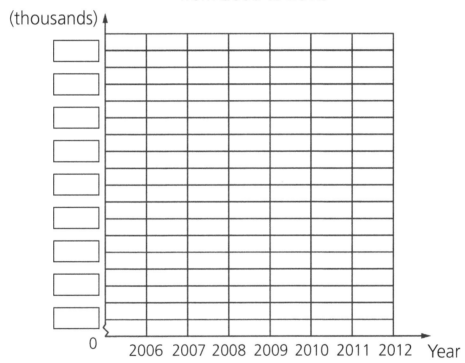

Graph showing private car ownership in Shanghai from 2006 to 2012

a. Between 2006 and 2012, the biggest rise in car ownership in Shanghai was between the year ( ) and the year ( ).

b. Using the line graph, try to analyse the development of private car ownership in Shanghai in this period.

_____

c. Given this situation, what advice would you give to the city's traffic control officer?

_____

3. Multiple choice – write the letter of the correct answer in the brackets.

If a is a natural number that is more than 11 but less than 19, then the average of the three numbers a, 8, and 12 could be (   ).

A. 10   **B.** 11   **C.** 13   **D.** 14

4. Fill in the brackets.

a. Alex, Dylan, Poppy and Emma go to the photo studio. If the four of them stand in a row, there are (   ) different possible ways they can stand.

b. Alex's Science score is 7.5 points lower than the average score for Science, Maths and English, and his Maths score is 9 points higher than the average score for the three subjects, so his English score is (   ) points lower than his Maths score.

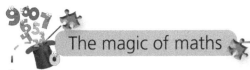

The magic of guessing a number

Poppy draws out a grid of 11 squares, as shown below.

'No matter which two numbers you choose, I can use my magic to guess the result,' Poppy said mysteriously to Dylan.

The magic steps:

a. Dylan chooses two numbers from 1 to 10 at random, and fills in the 1st and 2nd squares.

b. Starting from the 3rd square, Dylan fills in each box with the sum of the two numbers in the previous two squares until the 10th square is filled.

c. Dylan says the number in the 10th box.

d. What should be entered in the 11th box? (Note: Poppy has not seen the numbers Dylan has written in the nine boxes.)

Poppy turns her back to Dylan, takes out her calculator and does a quick calculation.

Something magic happens, and Poppy tells him the answer!

Think about how this works.

(You can discuss this trick with your family and classmates. An explanation of the maths behind the magic can be found on page 51 of this book.)